Roman

National Museum Wales Books

First published in 2012 by
Amgueddfa Cymru – National
Museum Wales, Cathays Park,
Cardiff, CF10 3NP, Wales

© National Museum of Wales

ISBN 978-0-7200-0619-3

Text: Adrian Pepper, Eloise Stanton
Design: Gill Advertising
Editor: Mari Gordon
Also available in Welsh as *Gemau
Rhufeinig*, ISBN 978-0-7200-0620-9

Contents

Foreword

Between the first and third centuries AD, a Roman Legion established a fortress on what is now Caerleon in south Wales. The Romans called it Isca, after the river Usk. The fortress became the home of the Second Augustan Legion, and was inhabited by some 5,000 soldiers at any one time. These men lived, laughed, fought and died in Isca and the surrounding area, and the personal objects and artefacts they left behind make up the foundation of the collection on display at the National Roman Legion Museum.

Discovering the gems

Archaeologists are aware that drains provide a perfect trap for lost possessions. For Roman soldiers, the fortress baths were a retreat to get clean after a hard day, as well as being a good place for social gathering and game playing.

During excavations of Caerleon fortress in the 1970s, archaeologists discovered a large covered channel underneath the floor of the bathhouse, which drained the various bathing pools. This drain contained an astonishing collection of eighty-eight remarkably engraved, semi-precious gemstones. The gems had all been lost sometime between AD 75 and 230. The Romans called these gemstones *Intaglios*, which means engraving or carving. This find ranks among the largest collection of gemstones to be found anywhere in the Roman Empire. Later, in the excavations of 1979, many tons of rubbish were washed through a fine sieve, revealing a magnificent range of finds from food-debris and glass to pottery, coins and other objects that had been lost or discarded by the Roman bathers. In the process of searching through the debris, more of these fascinating gemstones appeared.

Today, the collection is in excess of 110 individual gems, many of which are now on display at the National Roman Legion Museum.

The gemstones were set into rings of silver, bronze or iron, using natural adhesives such as resin or bitumen. General wear, combined with the humid atmosphere of the bathhouse, could loosen the stones, causing them to be detached from the rings and lost in the drainage system. We believe that even though the Romans knew they could sometimes lose their gemstones while bathing, they still wore them in order to keep away harmful supernatural influences, which they felt more at risk from while naked.

Romans believed that certain gemstones and rings brought them luck with the board games they played like *ludus latrunculorum*, a game very similar to today's checkers. They also used gemstones as signets for sealing documents and letters.

The ring below is made of silver and has a red jasper stone. The ring on the left is made of iron and is set with a cornelian stone depicting Minerva holding a winged Victory. Both rings show gemstones in their original settings.

Take a closer look

The Sol gemstone, about AD 160–230 (heliotrope)

This gemstone is engraved with an image of the Roman sun god *Sol* – sol is the Latin word for sun. He is shown wearing a crown that represents rays of sunlight. The Romans believed that Sol drove the chariot of the sun across the sky every day, pulled by four horses, and the gemstone shows Sol resting his whip over his left shoulder.

The Romans loved Greek art and culture; they even adopted the Greek gods as their own, but gave them different names. This intaglio is made of a stone called heliotrope, which presumably the gem cutter chose because it is named after Helios, the Greek god of the sun. The stone itself is black with flecks of red, which were thought to be rays of sunlight captured within.

13

Clasped Hands, about AD 160–230
(cornelian or sard)

This gemstone is engraved with
two hands clasped, which is a
symbol of unity. In Roman times
a woman would agree to be
married by holding hands with
her future husband in public, and
an important part of the wedding
ceremony centred on the couple
clasping each other's right hands.

Symbols, about AD 75–85
(amethyst)

This gemstone is a very pale
amethyst. It shows a *cornucopia*
or horn of plenty, which is a
symbol of abundance, a parrot
perched on a basket, and a poppy
head. Poppies were used for
medicinal purposes as they could
be made into painkillers and help
induce sleep.

Symbols, about AD 75–85 (agate)

A pair of scales is shown balancing on a *modius*, which was a vessel used for measuring grain. Some wheat is sprouting from the *modius*, which is closely associated with Ceres, the Roman goddess of the harvest. The bird sitting on top of the scales is a raven, which was thought to possess powers of prophecy, and the Romans sometimes taught them to say words and phrases.

Gods and goddesses

Diana, about AD 160–230
(cornelian)

Diana, goddess of the hunt, is
shown reaching to her quiver
for an arrow. The gemstone is
engraved with the initials B, E and
T, possibly the initials of the owner.
They are cut in reverse so they
would read correctly when it was
pressed into wax.

Minerva, about AD 85–100/110
(nicolo)

Minerva was the goddess of
wisdom and war, and was seen as
a protector of soldiers. Her image
would have been a popular choice
at Isca. She is wearing a helmet
and carrying a spear and shield
over her shoulder.

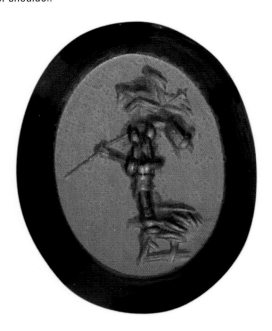

Jupiter, about AD 160–230
(cornelian)

Jupiter, the greatest and most
powerful of the Roman gods, is
shown seated on a throne. He is
holding a spear and a bowl. An
eagle, the symbol of the Roman
Empire and an animal commonly
associated with Jupiter, stands at
his feet.

Victory, about AD 160–230
(cornelian)

An image of the goddess of Victory
would have been particularly
appropriate as a signet for a
legionary soldier, as it signifies
the success of the Roman army.
Victory is a winged goddess and
is shown flying. She is holding a
wreath, which symbolises victory,
and a palm frond, which is an
emblem of peace.

Mars, about AD 160–230 (cornelian)

The god Mars is shown wearing
a helmet and carrying a spear,
reflecting his role as the god
of war.

Bonus Eventus, about AD 160–230 (red jasper)

Bonus Eventus literally translates as 'The Bearer of Good Things'. Gods and goddesses who personified good health and prosperity were common on gemstones. *Bonus Eventus* was god of agriculture and the harvest.

Here he is seen wearing a wreath on his head and balancing a shepherd's crook on his shoulder, from which hang a cooking pan and a dead hare.

Animals

Gemstones show carvings of many different animals. They were likely to be linked to forms of transport, agriculture, food supply, hunting, religion, pets and fond memories. The soldiers that lived at Isca would have bought a gemstone ring that was affordable to them. As representations of animals are so common, it is thought they were simpler to produce, which would have brought down the cost of the engraving.

These animals had many meanings for the Romans, here are just a few:

Ibis were closely associated with Egypt, as they were sacred to the Egyptian goddess Isis. During the reign of Emperor Hadrian Egypt was a province of Rome, and commemorative coins were produced with various Egyptian symbols, including the Ibis, on the back.

Parrots were usually of Indian origin. They were seen as companions or pets, as they chattered like humans.

Hares were seen as food and are often shown being devoured by other animals, like eagles or foxes.

Donkeys/pack asses were considered as stupid and were commonly used for ploughing and carrying loads for agricultural purposes.

Goat's hair and skins were used for making rough country clothes, they supplied milk and this was then made into cheese.

Foxes were connected to a religious rite re-enacted every year on 19 April in honour of the goddess Ceres in Rome.

Horses were used for war,
transport, racing in the circus,
hunting, pulling vehicles and
chariots, farm and factory work.

Red jasper gemstones

Red jasper is an opaque stone that is rich in colour and has a very smooth and shiny surface.
It was found in the highland areas of Britain and the Alps, around lakes, streams and mountains, and was more readily available than other stones.

By the third century, as Roman fashion changes, red jaspers and cornelian gemstones dominate the group. It was believed that red jasper had magical properties. However, images engraved on some of these beautiful gems often seem oddly child-like. Imagine, for example, these rings worn by brave, strong Roman soldiers about to go to battle, yet when we look closely we see their rings show images of hobby horses, parrots or goats!

Eagle, about AD 85–100/110 (sard)

The eagle was the symbol of the Roman Empire, and a common theme on gemstones. Each Roman Legion carried a golden 'standard', a long pole with badges or flags on it, formed in the shape of an eagle, called an *Aquila*. When a Legion was on the march the *Aquila* was carried in front by a soldier called an *Aquilifer*. Loss of the eagle standard during battle brought great shame on the Roman army, which went to great lengths to protect it or recover it if lost. The emblem of the eagle appears not just on gemstones, but also frequently throughout the Roman world, for example on sculptures and coinage.

Crescent moon and stars,
about AD 160–230 (citrine)

This gemstone is engraved with
an image of a crescent moon
containing one star, surrounded
by six others. This motif was
especially popular during the
reign of Emperor Hadrian (AD
117–138), and appears a lot on
coins from that era. It could
symbolise a pattern of stars
known as the Seven Sisters. The
Romans believed the god Atlas
was forced to carry the heavens
on his shoulders, so Jupiter turned
his seven daughters into stars to
comfort him. It may also represent
the sun, moon and five planets that
were known to the Romans at
this time.

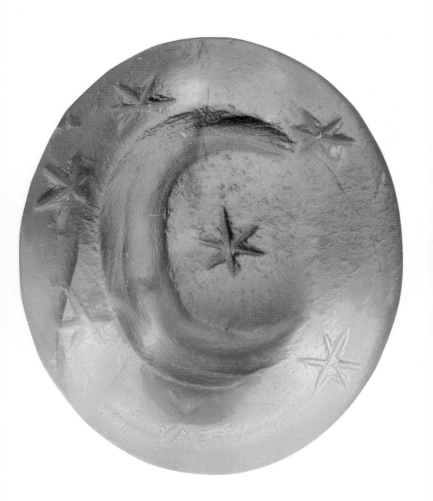

Alexander the Great,
second to third century AD
(red jasper)

As well as the collection of
gemstones found at the fortress
baths, other examples have
been found in Caerleon. This one
was found in the amphitheatre,
during Sir Mortimer Wheeler's
excavations in the 1920s. This
beautiful gemstone shows an
image of the classical hero
Alexander the Great, wearing a
helmet with a crest.

39

The gem cutters' art

Semi-precious stones came from all corners of the Roman Empire and beyond. Some, such as jasper and crystal, could be found in Britain, but most came from places much further afield, such as Egypt, Crete and even India.

Blank gemstones were shaped from the raw material ready for engraving. The gem cutter's primary tool was called a lathe. It consisted of a metal disc roughened with emery powder mixed with oil, attached to a spindle. This was then rotated to engrave the gem, either using a hand-held bow or a foot-peddle called a treadle. Pressing glass paste into a mould made cheap, imitation gemstones.

Gem cutters must have had remarkable eyesight, and there is no evidence of any magnifying aids being used. However some may have been short-sighted, and there is evidence of children being trained to cut gems.

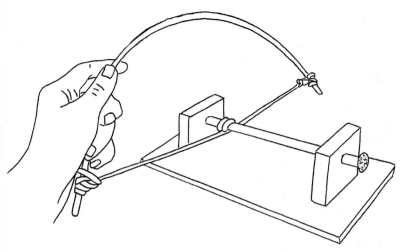

An illustration of a Roman-style lathe

An Indian-style lathe, used today

This photograph shows gemstones
being cut and shaped in India,
where traditional methods are
still in use.

Some personal favourites

After studying the gemstones, the
authors would like to share some
favourites with you.

Adrian:
I love the Alexander gemstone, as it shows so much detail, right down to the definition, strength and masculinity of this heroic figure. The stone red jasper is also one of my favourite stones – it has such a distinctive colouring and beautiful looking surface.

Eloise:

The citrine intaglio with the crescent moon and stars is beautiful. It's only 10 millimetres in width and the engraving is tiny but it looks so perfect it's unbelievable to think it was created with no magnification.

As an amateur astronomer, one of my favourite constellations is the Pleides. It's very humbling to think that when this was engraved two thousand years ago, the Romans looked up and saw the same patterns in the night sky that we do today.

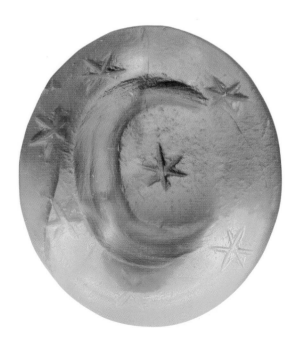

**If you'd like to see the gemstones
for yourself, visit the National
Roman Legion Museum. Tell us
which one is your favourite!**

The National Roman Legion
Museum, High Street, Caerleon,
NP18 1AE, tel. (029) 20573550.
Open Monday–Saturday
10am–5pm; Sunday 2pm–5pm.

To see more mineral specimens,
visit National Museum Cardiff.

National Museum Cardiff, Cathays
Park, Cardiff CF10 3NP,
tel. (029) 20397951. Open Tuesday–
Sunday 10am–5pm.

References

Catherine Johns, *The Jewellery of Roman Britain* (1996)

Catherine Johns, *The Snettisham Roman Jeweller's Hoard* (1997)

John Edward Lee, *Isca Silurum: an Illustrated Catalogue of the Museum* (1862)

Jack Ogden, *Jewellery of the Ancient World* (1982)

J. M. C. Toynbee, *Animals in Roman Life and Art* (1973)

David Zienkiewicz, *The Legionary Fortress Baths at Caerleon: The Finds* (1986)

David Zienkiewicz, *Roman Gems from Caerleon* (1987)

Wales's national museums

Amgueddfa Cymru is a family of seven museums located throughout Wales. Each family member gives a unique and vivid experience of Wales's history, while sharing the Amgueddfa Cymru values of excellence and learning.

The National Roman Legion Museum
Caerleon, Newport

The National Wool Museum
Dre-fach Felindre, Carmarthenshire

The National Waterfront Museum
Maritime Quarter, Swansea

National Museum Cardiff
Cathays Park, Cardiff

St Fagans: National History Museum
St Fagans, Cardiff

Big Pit: National Coal Museum
Blaenafon, Torfaen

The National Slate Museum
Llanberis, Gwynedd

Find out more about the 'hidden' collections on our website Rhagor – www.museumwales.ac.uk/Rhagor